RACE
AROUND THE
SUN

First Edition

WALT HARPER

To order additional copies of this book, contact:
Xlibris
1-888-795-4274
www.Xlibris.com
Orders@Xlibris.com

ISBN:	Softcover		978-1-7960-9590-6
		Hardcover		978-1-7960-9591-3
		EBook		978-1-7960-9589-0

Library of Congress Control Number:	2020905774

Print information available on the last page

Rev. date: 05/15/2020

There are many dedications required for such a broad topic. I kept it at a minimal to make it, hopefully!, amenable to the reader.

I dedicate this book to all the brave souls that dared to depart from the only planet we have ever known and all of the workers who made it possible to explore.

I also dedicate this book to my Mom, Mallie Harper, because she was the only person who would take to me to the airport for me to learn how to fly.

Lastly, I dedicate this book to Wikipedia.org and its many divisions that enabled me to research the necessary information required to truthfully tell this tale of people actually striving for a worthwhile goal.

TABLE OF CONTENTS

Foreword

The 21st Century started without many substantial events but then it quickly accelerated. Within the realm of Space Exploration, the 21st Century might very well become epic and lead to unimaginable advances in the Sciences, as well as, Human Development.

Discreetly, private Space Companies, particularly Blue Origins and SpaceX, became established and began building rockets of their own criteria. Both companies made bold predictions that were difficult to believe and both companies accomplished phenomenal successes very rapidly. Despite the complexities of Space Exploration, both companies were able to employ the pools of talented scientists needed and proceed without the conflicts of politics or war.

With the full cooperation of NASA and the continued health of the American Economy, Blue Origin developed the New Shepherd Rocket and SpaceX developed the Falcon 1 Rocket. Each rocket used a similar technology known as VTVL- Vertical Take-off and Vertical Landing- which would become the standard operating procedure for future rocket flights, but both companies have different strategies for the colonization of Space.

The recent urgency for Space Exploration might seem remarkable because it has dwindled since the 1960's, because simply because we love to explore. Space Exploration has never before had as good of an opportunity as this. It will continue undauntedly until our curiosity is satisfied.

In any situation, the universal benefits of our quest to explore Space has improved our general health and outlook. Our history of many previous, though less complicated, explorations have proven this to be true. The hardships of nearly all prior explorations have been endured and minimalized in memory.

The increase in general optimism alone is sufficient motivation to continue Space Exploration. Advances in Mathematics and Physics are sure to result and there is no greater purpose for our many scientists and dreamers to pursue. The mysteries which have existed for all time have waited very patiently for our discovery of them.

CHAPTER 1

Intersection of Orbits

Earth is a busy planet.

It has an orbit around the Sun of about 584,000,000 miles and it travels that far in about a year which has about 8760 hours. Those two approximate figures result in Earth having an orbital speed of 30 km/s which equals about 67,000 mph (Velocity = Distance/ Time).

Mars is Earth's nearest companion planet with an orbital distance of about 892,212,314 miles around the Sun. Mars orbits the Sun once every 687 Earth days therefore, Mars has an orbital speed of about 24 km/s which equals about 53,686 mph.

The difference in orbital speed between these two planets is 6 km/sec, or 13,314 mph, with Mars being the slower planet on a much longer orbit. Mars and Earth converge once every 26 months when the distance between Mars and Earth diminishes from nearly 400,000,000 miles to less than 90,000,000 miles.

The last convergent moment was July 27, 2018 and the next convergent moment will be October 13, 2020. Our best convergence might by July 27, 2028 when our technology and ability coincide with Mars' proximity.

There is much delight knowing that we are on the faster planet, yet, we also have much delight from other factors over Mars, like air, water, and climates that enable plants to grow.

The total number of delights about Earth over Mars might never be fully calculated and why should they? We are definitely on the better planet!

In the past 170,000 years of human history (that figure will always be debated!), we've only counted the past 2100 years, or so, with positive numbers. That calculates as 1.235% of human History with 98.765% of human History undocumented and essentially irrelevant, at least, and insofar, as our History has become flattering and documented by us.

I dread to ponder when Human History we would have started had it not been for the Advent of Christ! Other worldly events were lesser known.

Of all these orbits around the Sun (estimate around 4,500,000,000 Earth orbits of which we, as a species, witnessed much less than .01%!), our own Moon became a goal within the Twentieth Century and Mars became a goal within this Twenty-First Century. Ambition to explore Space became manifest in the first decade of the Twentieth Century and substantial progress in Space Exploration is expected in the Twenty-First Century.

As of the Early Twenty-First Century, the planetary goal for the Twenty-Second Century has not yet been determined, however, it is anticipated to be farther away from the Sun than Mars but not by much. Mars is pretty cold at -81° Fahrenheit and the International Space Station fluctuates between +250° F and -250° F.

In any event, we have much time to decide upon the next planetary goal on our next Race around the Sun.

CHAPTER 2

Founders of Space Programs

The Founder of the American Space Program

Dr. Robert Hutchings Goddard
(b. October 5, 1882-d. August 10, 1945).

Dr. Robert Goddard is the American credited with the launching of the first liquid-fueled rocket on March 16, 1926 so, therefore, the future of all Space Programs became established from that time.

Dr. Goddard's work suffered from lack of Federal funding, his ailments of tuberculosis, and general ambivalence for new sciences, however, the benefits of his early work persist in modern times.

Dr. Goddard was a genius with 214 patents; more than half of which were filed after his demise by his widow, Mrs. Esther Christine Goddard. Although Dr. Goddard kept meticulous records of his work and published several important technical papers, he was very secretive about the progress he had made and never tried to garner fame.

Dr. Goddard is well known for his event that happened on October 19, 1899 which is known as the "Cherry Tree Dream". 17-year-old Goddard climbed a Cherry tree to trim dead limbs and became inspired by the sky.

After climbing down from the tree, he wrote the following;

"On this day, I climbed a tall cherry tree behind the barn..and as I looked to the fields at the east, I imagined how wonderful it would be to make some device which had even the possibility of ascending to Mars, and how it would look on a small scale, if sent up from the meadow at my feet. I have several photographs of the tree, taken since, with the little ladder I made to climb it, leaning against it.

It seemed to me then that a weight whirling around a horizontal shaft, moving more rapidly above than below, could furnish lift by virtue of the greater centrifugal force at the top of the path.

I was a different boy when I descended the tree from when I ascended. Existence at last seemed very purposive."

From that day forward, Dr. Goddard observed October 19th as a personal Anniversary Day of his greatest inspiration.

His inspiration stayed with him for his entire life, but he was somewhat impeded by his frail health. He spent his time away from high school in the local public library and learned of Samuel Langley's research on aeronautics as published by the Smithsonian magazine. The articles piqued his curiosity.

Young Goddard began observing birds, particularly swallows and chimney swifts that have excellent flying abilities. He studied them well enough to supposition that they had intelligence to change their body orientation to control flight. He compiled his findings and, in 1901 at the age of 19, he wrote the Editor of St. Nicholas magazine.

The Editor rebuffed young Goddard's manuscript, citing that *"machines will not act with such intelligence."*. Young Goddard would not accept this declination of his first paper gracefully. He prevailed over short-sightedness and wrote many more papers.

He was held back two full years in High School because of his health before graduating in 1901 as the Class President and Valedictorian. After recuperation, his ambitions were apparently keener than most.

There, he gave a speech indicative of his aspirations called "Taking Things for Granted". It contained the following quotes;

Just as in the sciences, we have learned that we are too ignorant to safely pronounce anything impossible, so for the individual, since we cannot know just what are his limitations, we can hardly say with certainty that anything is within or beyond his grasp. Each must remember that no one can predict to what heights of wealth, fame, or usefulness he may rise until he has honestly endeavored, and he should derive courage from the fact that all sciences have been, at some time, in the same condition as he, and that it has often proved true that the dream of yesterday is the hope of today and the reality of tomorrow."

Young Goddard stayed in his hometown of Worcester, Massachusetts and enrolled in Worcester Polytechnic Institution where he graduated with a B.S. degree in Physics in 1908. He stayed and worked there as an Instructor of Physics for another year.

In the fall of 1909, he enrolled at Clark University in Worcester, Massachusetts, attained his Ph.D. in Physics, and taught as an honorary fellow. He remained loyal to Clark University for many years until World War II interrupted his professorship there.

In 1912, Dr. Goddard moved to Princeton University's Palmer Physical Laboratory and accepted a research fellowship. Soon thereafter, he fell ill to a serious bout of tuberculosis and returned to Worcester.

Although bed-ridden and under the care of a nurse, Dr. Goddard continued his work on liquid-fueled rocket theory, learned of intellectual property, and secured his first patent in October 1913. He became upset once when the nurse tried to tidy up his papers and he told her, "*I have to live to do this work*."-such was his zeal for his fate.

He returned to work at Clark University as a Physics Professor in late 1914 and began to build a solid fueled rocket. When he launched the rocket on campus grounds, the commotion was so intense that he promised to move his experiments into the Physics Laboratory which also was unsatisfactory.

Dr. Goddard settled on using his Aunt Effie's farm in Auburn, Massachusetts as the nation's only rocket test laboratory but this site also disturbed the neighbors. Rocket testing continued for many years with contributions sent in by the Smithsonian Institution who learned of Dr. Goddard's rocket research and funded a $5,000, 5-year grant in 1916. The National Geographic Society and The Aero Club of America also contributed. Even Clark University donated $3500 and access to their machine shop. It appeared that liquid fueled rockets would become discovered!

Then disaster struck!

The Great Depression of October 1929 happened without notice and the entire Country was swept into financial ruin. Even the fantastic accomplishments of Dr. Goddard's 1920 Rocket flights were in peril of never being expanded upon.

As fate would have it, Dr. Goddard's research attracted the attention of Colonel Charles Lindbergh through the New York Times newspaper and he became an advocate. Col. Lindbergh was concerned about the future of aviation, was interested in rocket propulsion, and was, undeniably, the World's most famous aviator at that time.

Col. Lindbergh checked out Dr. Goddard's credentials before introducing himself over the phone in November 1929. He then met with Dr. Goddard at Clark University and was impressed with the amount of progress already made. They formed a lifelong alliance!

By using his personal charm and celebrity, Col. Lindbergh was able to approach Mr. Daniel Guggenheim of the famous Guggenheim Foundation and represent Mr. Goddard's dire situation. With the whole of Space Exploration dependent on that meeting and the Depression worsening, Col. Lindbergh produced a miracle!

Mr. Guggenheim became thoroughly convinced of the future of Space Exploration by Col. Lindbergh and donated the very extravagant sum of $100,000 over the next four years. Future financial support would be sustained by Mr. Harry Guggenheim, his son.

The importance of the Guggenheim Foundation to all of every Space Program can never be depreciated! Although most of the United States would suffer misery for years, our original Space Program and all the advantages it promised remained steadfast in our future.

Assuredly, Space Exploration did little for profit potential then but, nearly a Century later, all of us benefit from Dr. Goddard's work daily.

With the new funding provided, The Goddard's and a few friends from Clark University moved to a remote town named Roswell, New Mexico and set up shop. A meteorologist suggested Roswell as having good weather for both rocket research and Dr. Goddard's health, but the isolation was also desirable too. After the local people confirmed that their privacy concerns were nearly the same as his, the decision to move there was finalized.

Work at Roswell proceeded until The Depression caught up with them in 1932 and funding was temporarily delayed for two years. Dr. Goddard abandoned Roswell and reluctantly returned to Clark University and his employment as a Physics Professor. The prospects for his continued research were indefinite.

In the fall of 1934, Dr. Goddard and crew returned to Roswell and resumed work. His experiments with gyroscopic stabilization and steering were successful and different fuels were tried to increase efficiencies. He started experiments in series of rockets; beginning with Series A rockets in 1935 and ending with Series P rockets in 1941 when the Second World War required Dr. Goddard to abandon Roswell again and assist with the War Effort.

In October 1938, Major (later General Officer) Jimmy Doolittle visited Dr. Goddard at Roswell. He quickly grasped the concepts of rocket propulsion and the capabilities of rockets at war but was unable to persuade the Pentagon to pursue rocket development. The Pentagon instead pursued nuclear weapons with the Manhattan Project because the Nazis were suspected of doing the same.

Before leaving Roswell, New Mexico in 1941, Dr. Goddard achieved a maximum altitude of 8,900 feet with a L-13 rocket, whereas the Nazis had reached a maximum altitude of 577,427 feet with a V-2 rocket the next year. Dr. Goddard was constrained to using gasoline and liquid oxygen for fuel while the Nazis had developed a fuel consisting of ethanol and water coupled with liquid oxygen. Strategies differed, in that Dr. Goddard concentrated on controllability of the rocket and directional control in Space. The Nazis' only motivation for rockets was as an expendable weapon.

Several of Dr. Goddard's designs used in the A-4 Rocket were adopted by Professor Hermann Oberth of Nazi Germany and used in the V-2 Rocket during World War II. Professor Oberth, Germany's pioneer of rocketry, had requested and received technical papers from Dr. Goddard in 1919.

Although space flight was not considered until 31 years later, after the Soviet launch of Sputnik on October 4, 1957, Dr. Goddard's first rockets demonstrated the basic principles of rocketry that are still used today. Dr. Goddard recognized his work when he first saw Dr. von Braun's work on the V-2 Rocket at Annapolis, Maryland in 1945.

The Russians also benefitted from Dr. Goddard's research in Rocketry through a spy who worked at the U. S. Navy Bureau of Aeronautics in 1935. How much the Russians learned of Dr. Goddard's work is not well known although it's safe to say that at one time in History everyone who was interested in Rocketry depended on Dr. Robert Goddard for their start.

Dr. Goddard suffered from the weather in Maryland where he worked for the Navy during World War II. He eventually developed throat cancer, was treated in Baltimore, Maryland, and died on August 10, 1945. He is buried in Worcester, Massachusetts; the town where his life began 62 years previous.

Dr. Goddard's widow, Mrs. Esther Christine Goddard, alongside the Guggenheim Foundation, sued the U.S. Armed Forces for prior patent infringement in 1951. A $1,000,000 settlement was divided equally by both parties in 1960. That was, at the time, the largest settlement awarded by the U.S. Court and more than the total cost of all funding for all of Dr. Goddard's work.

The Founder of the French Space Program

**Robert Albert Charles Esnault-Pelterie,
(b. November 8, 1881-d. December 6, 1957).**

Monsieur Robert Esnault-Pelterie was France's Founder of its Space Program who in 1913 produced a paper that defined the "Rocket Equation" and proposed Moon and planetary travel. He did not know of Tsiolkovsky's earlier work and developed rockets independently.

His original intent was to develop ballistic missiles for the French War Department in 1929. Sadly, two years later, a rocket experiment using tetranitromethane fuel exploded and he lost three fingers from his right hand. He ended his exploration of rockets soon thereafter and France, as a Nation, failed to further pursue rocket science.

The legacy of Monsieur Esnault-Pelterie includes his military career as an officer in World War I, his education as an aircraft engineer, designer of the aileron, joystick, and other aircraft controls, as well as being a famous theorist of astronautics and space travel. Early on in 1906, he flew a towed glider for about 1,600 ft and, in the following year, he flew his first powered aircraft.

He and Andre-Louis Hirsch, a Parisian banker, also established the first organization in the World to honor astronautics-The Societe Astronomique de France (The French Astronomy Society) on December 26, 1927. The French Society of Astronomy awarded its highest award-The Prix Jules Janssen-to innovators of rocketry and space exploration.

In 1930, Monsieur Esnault-Pelterie wrote L'Astronautique and was awarded the Prix Jules Janssen for his rocket research. He went on to become inducted into the inaugural class of The International Space Hall of Fame.

The Founder of the German Space Program

Hermann Julius Oberth
(b. June 25, 1894-d. December 25, 1989).

Dr. Hermann Oberth began his career as a Medical Doctor but his studies were interrupted by World War I. As an infantryman in the Imperial German Army, he was sent to the Eastern Front to fight the Russians.

After the war, Dr. Oberth returned to Romania where he worked in a Hospital, married, and started a family. At the same time, his natural curiosity about rocketry prompted him to design and present a ballistic missile design to the Prussian Minister of War. It was rejected.

Resolutely, Dr. Oberth moved to Munich in 1919 and enrolled to study physics and mathematics. He graduated in 1922 but his doctoral dissertation was rejected as being "utopian".

About the same time, Dr. Oberth wrote a highly controversial book called, "The Rocket into Planetary Space" and another one called, "Ways to Spaceflight". His notoriety as a Rocket Scientist became established and he was employed as a consultant for the movie, "The Woman in the Moon". Rockets and spaceflight became popularized in Germany.

Yet, Dr. Oberth was far more than a movie consultant! He contacted Dr. Goddard in the United States, asked for, and received a copy of Dr. Goddard's 1919 Technical Report on Liquid Fueled Rockets. This report must have aided Dr. Oberth in his first static firing of a liquid fueled rocket in 1929. A young student present at that first firing was none other than soon-to-be Professor Wernher von Braun!

Founder of America's National Space Program

Wernher Magnus Maximillian, Freiherr von Braun,
(b. March 23, 1912-d. June 16, 1977)

Dr. Wernher von Braun was as curious as any other Founder of Space Programs, beginning early in his youth. He had an instinctive curiosity for astronomy which he explored with a gifted telescope. He was also good as a musician with the piano and he composed music.

Herr von Braun's inquisitiveness was boundless and included land speed records made by rocket-propelled cars. They looked so simple and took off so fast! This one experiment would eventually get him in trouble at the early age of 12!

Without adult assistance, steadfast young von Braun fastened fireworks to his toy wagon and set off to accomplish his own land speed record with fireworks, a.k.a., solid fueled rockets. Things got out of control and his toy wagon was destroyed. Young Wernher was essentially unharmed but taken into Police custody. His father arrived and arranged for him to be released.

That incident may have been the reason Herr Wernher von Braun was always adamant about planning, safety testing, redundant systems, and training. To his credit, accidents were few and the American Space Program was reasonably safe despite the dangerous nature of Rocketry. With German precision and attention to detail, he directed the American Space Program safely all the way through Apollo 11 and Man's first step on the Moon on July 20, 1969.

Herr Wernher von Braun studied at the finest schools in Germany but initially did not apply himself to his studies. It wasn't until later when he read Professor Herman Oberth's book, "The Rocket into Planetary Space" that he developed the discipline to study Mathematics and Physics that, in turn, satisfied his interest in space travel.

In 1930, Herr von Braun moved to Berlin and joined The Spaceflight Society. He continued his education at Technische Hochschule and graduated in 1932 with a diploma in Mechanical Engineering.

While there, he collaborated with Professor Oberth and his associate, Herr Willy Ley, on liquid fueled rocket engines. He then understood that his diploma wasn't sufficient to do design work on Rockets.

From there, he attended the Freidrich-Wilhelm University of Berlin and graduated with a doctorate in Physics in 1934. Dr. von Braun was well on his way to designing rockets, mainly for military purposes, when Nazi Germany interfered.

Although Dr. von Braun voluntarily joined the Nazi Party in 1937, he disliked politics and remained engrossed with his work at Peenemunde, Germany-the German National Center for Rocket Development. There, he researched what Dr. Goddard had accomplished with his A-4 Rocket and tried to replicate it.

As the World War II progressed, Dr. von Braun was recruited as a Lieutenant in the SS of the Nazi Party. He hesitated and sought advice from his superior, General Dornberger, who assured Dr. von Braun that he would lose favor, possibly his job as Technical Director, if he did not oblige. Dr. von Braun accepted without full awareness of what the new position would entail.

Dr. von Braun's work on the A-4 Rocket was excellent and it was renamed the V-2 Rocket; the "V" stood for Vengeance. The rocket was, by far, the most formidable weapon of World War II and had the ability to steer towards any target by means of an Inertial Guidance System. It attacked at supersonic speed (1790 mph) and delivered nearly a ton of ordnance (2,010 lbs.).

Fuehrer Adolf Hitler became enthralled by it and used the V-2 Rocket to its maximum war utility as a weapon and also as a propaganda device. He used the V-2 Rocket to boost the morale of Nazi Germany as the war was turning against them and grandly hoped it would defeat his enemies, causing them to surrender. Hitler's aspirations for his rocket program exceeded his aspirations for his Army and Navy combined!

The grimmest aspect of the Nazi Rocket Program was its use of slave labor. Thousands of slaves expired from exhaustion or were killed at the Dora Concentration Camp or Mittelwork Factory that built the V-2 Rocket. Hitler was desperate, resources were getting scarce, and the most heinous acts were dealt upon the prisoners.

At least one of SS Major von Braun's associates was found guilty of war crimes though he, himself, never was accused. SS Major Wernher von Braun learned of plans to move his staff away from Peenemunde, Germany and assemble them in a nearby town as the War was ending. He suspected that because Rocket Scientists were valuable war assets they would be gathered up and killed. He was able to persuade the SS commander to disperse the Peenemunde staff then made his own way back to Austria where he arranged his own surrender to the American side.

On May 2, 1945, SS Major Wernher von Braun voluntarily surrendered to American Forces and was immediately taken into custody as a prisoner of Operation Overcast, later renamed Operation Paperclip.

He and seven hundred of his fellow scientists were well-known to Army Intelligence so the U.S. Secretary of State approved their transfer to the United States, specifically Ft. Bliss, Texas. Professor von Braun disliked the conditions he was placed in and referred to his status as a "Prisoner of Peace".

His staff continued to greet him as "Herr Professor" and they were allowed to keep working on rockets under austere military conditions. U.S. Army officers ignored Professor von Braun's complaints about his living conditions and directed him forward into the Hermes Project where he worked on captured V-2 rockets. While there, he also trained military and civilian personnel in rocket science.

Professor von Braun returned to Germany, presumably with military escort, to marry Maria Luise von Quistorp on March 1, 1947. As a married couple, they returned to the U.S. along with his father and mother on March 26, 1947. They had three children.

Three years later, Professor von Braun, his family, and his team were relocated to Huntsville, Alabama which would be their home for the next twenty years. He and his team were assigned to design and build the Redstone rocket at the Redstone Arsenal for testing of delivery of a live nuclear warhead. The Redstone rocket was controlled by the first high-precision Inertial Guidance System and performed flawlessly.

Walt Harper

Professor von Braun became a naturalized citizen of the United States on April 15, 1955 and was promoted to the position of Director of the Development Operations Division of the Army Ballistic Missile Agency. War and its misery were firmly in his past.

The Russian launch of their satellite, Sputnik, on October 4, 1957 proved Russian superiority in the "Space Race" and startled the American Space Program. Unknown to the public, Professor von Braun, and his team had modified a Redstone rocket for exactly that purpose and named it Jupiter-C. Safety concerns prompted Professor von Braun to delay launching of the Jupiter-C Rocket at a time prior to the Sputnik launch, however, America's first satellite, Explorer 1, was launched on January 31, 1958, just four months later!

Justifiably, America's Space Program was improved significantly with a more distinct purpose and plan. It was removed from military bases and arsenals. Its new Base of Operations would be NASA-National Aeronautics and Space Administration-established July 29, 1958 by President Eisenhower signing The National Aeronautics and Space Act. Space Exploration became recognized as a challenge worthy of national interest!

The strategic advantages of operations in Space have always been obvious. Professor von Braun wrote of them often. He envisioned the launches of ballistic missiles from orbital platforms at will.

On December 20, 2019, President Trump made Professor von Braun's visions of space warfare more relevant when he established the United States Space Force. That might be a violation of the Outer Space Treaty signed on January 27, 1967 by United States President Lyndon Johnson. Of course, USSC has only intentions of National Defense.

On January 16, 1969, Professor von Braun confirmed that he would remain at Huntsville, Alabama and lead the Apollo Applications Program.

There had been talk of him becoming distracted by Disney movie production, satellite technology, biospheres, and many other topics associated with Space Exploration. Despite his notoriety and popularity, Professor von Braun remained loyal to the Saturn 5 Rocket Program being developed.

On March 1, 1970, Professor von Braun moved to Washington, DC to begin work as NASA's Deputy Associate Administrator for Planning. He did not enjoy the politics of DC and after several conflicts over budgets, goals, and similar details of management, he retired from NASA on May 26, 1972.

Retirement for Professor Wernher von Braun was brief because he was stricken with cancer and died on June 16, 1977. He is buried in Alexandria, Virginia.

Professor von Braun was elected to the National Academy of Engineering in 1967 and he was awarded twelve honorary doctorates. When he was awarded the National Medal of Science in 1977 at the White House, he was absent from the celebration because of his hospitalization.

Of the many accolades awarded to Professor von Braun, being recognized for his responsibility for engineering Apollo 11 and getting the first Lunar Lander on the Moon on July 20, 1969 must have been one of his favorites. His masterpiece, The Saturn 5 Rocket, remains the most powerful three stage rocket ever built as of 2020.

The Founder of the Russian Space Program

Konstatin Eduardovich Tsiolkovsky,
(b. September 17, 1857-d. September 19, 1935).

Mr. Konstatin Tsoilkovsky's biography precedes all biographies of space pioneers and is perhaps the most fascinating. His genius combined with his imagination and drive would leave permanent markers on all Space Programs that followed. His discoveries were the foundations of Space Exploration.

As far as the recorded history of space programs relate, his life precedes all other pioneers of space programs and his work was completely original. Despite having never seen a rocket nor delving in rocket experiments, his contributions would endure for all time.

Mr. Konstatin Tsiolkovsky lived in a log house near Kaluga, Russia, a small town about 120 miles southwest of Moscow. He lost much of his hearing to Scarlet Fever at the age of 10 and his Mother died when he was 13 years old. Life was hard for the young man.

He was denied elementary school enrollment because of his hearing disability and spent a lot of his time reading books. He became reclusive and somewhat anti-social as he individually studied engineering sciences, particularly Mathematics and Physics, at home. Konstatin was a teenager when he developed a curiosity for space travel.

Mr. Tsiolkovsky was a strong- willed person who traveled to libraries in Moscow to study anything there that involved the sciences. He read Jules Verne's books and conceived the idea of a Space Elevator there. He became further encouraged after meeting Nikolai Fyodorov, a fellow Russian with dreams of Space Exploration.

After 3 years of his self-study in Moscow libraries, his Father became concerned about his son's failing health and inability to provide for himself. He insisted that Konstatin return to Kaluga and assume a more responsible lifestyle. Konstatin obliged.

Despite the lack of a formal education, Mr. Tsiolkovsky passed the teacher's exam and began gainful employment as a Teacher. He also married and started a family. His hard work resulted in promotions to other teaching positions around Kaluga, yet he never could abandon his fascination with space travel.

At this time in History, transportation was primarily by horse-drawn wagons, rockets were about 40 years distant in the future, and Konstatin was a schoolteacher with an insatiable desire to reveal his philosophical observations of space travel. His genius persisted in conjunction with his job and he pursued his ambitions in the only avenue available-by designing experiments to prove his theories.

Around 1880, he completed his first scientific study, "Theory of Gases", in which he explained the kinetic energy of different gases and he submitted it to the Russian Physico-Chemical Society. The Society rejected it by stating that the information provided had been completed 25 years previous. Konstatin was disappointed but not discouraged.

His next scientific study, "The Mechanics of the Animal Organism" was favorably received by the Society. Konstatin was offered a membership into the Russian Physico-Chemical Society for this work which he accepted.

Although this last scientific study seems irrelevant for a Founder of a Space Program, it is testament to Mr. Tsiolkovsky's genius and another step towards his quest for rocket science for interplanetary travel. He appeased himself by exploring the possibility of morphing metal dirigibles-the only type of aviation (lighter-than-air) at that time. In that, Konstatin had no success but he continued on with his research of aerodynamics.

In 1897, Mr. Tsiolkovsky designed and built Russia's first wind tunnel in his apartment. With a grant from the Russian Academy of Sciences, he developed a system of measuring the drag coefficients of common geometric shapes. Airplanes wouldn't be invented for another six years and the experiments may have appeared purposeless, however, the science of Aerodynamics was first formed.

The information gleaned from the first Wind Tunnel attracted the attention of a Russian scientist named Nikolay Yegorovich Zhukovsky, the Father of Russian Aviation. Drag coefficents are still of engineering significance for everything from cars to rockets in these Modern Times.

Essentially, that title also belonged to Mr. Tsiolkovsky since he conceived metal dirigibles and heavier-than-air aircraft with metal frames. All early aircraft were wooden framed; the first metal airplane didn't get built by Hugo Junkers until 1915 -the J 1. Metal aircraft proved successful and it was the only construction type used in the Second World War.

Mr. Tsiolkovsky's premier accomplishment occurred in May 1903 when he published, "Exploration of Outer Space by Means of Rocket Devices"-an epic dissertation for anyone studying the History of interplanetary travel! That publication preceded all other works concerning Rocketry by several decades.

Eight years later in 1911, he published the second section of "Exploration of Outer Space by Means of Rocket Devices". In it, he calculated what's known as "Escape Velocity" from Earth's gravity and the minimum velocity for a rocket to maintain horizontal orbital speed around Earth-5 miles per second-even though no rocket existed!

His life's work culminated in "Tsiolkovsky's Equation" and it is written as such:

$$\Delta \upsilon = \upsilon e \; \ln (mo \div mf)$$

Where:
$\Delta \upsilon$ = change in rocket acceleration speed
υe = exhaust velocity of the engine(s)
mo/mf = initial mass (mo) and final mass (mf) of the rocket.

He recorded his equation on May 10, 1897. Coincidently, a similar equation was recorded in the same year by Russian mathematician, I.V. Meshchersky as "Dynamics of a Point of Variable Mass".

Mr. Tsiolkovsky designed a three-stage rocket, an airlock, and many other components that would, someday, be used for interplanetary travel after that conception became acceptable. He even designed a hovercraft. His engineering excellence was as boundless as his imagination.

In 1914, he grew tired of continuing his unrequited campaign of exploring aeronautics and astronautics. He instead turned his talents towards another unsolvable problem-alleviating poverty.

World War 1 was soon followed by the Bolshevik Revolution and Mr. Tsiolkovsky did not gain under a Communist rule. His sole award for a lifetime of science was admission to the Socialist Academy in 1918. He continued as a High School Mathematics Teacher until his retirement at age 63. He never left Kaluga and he died there after an operation for stomach cancer two years later in 1935.

It is unknown how much of Dr. Goddard's research with liquid-fueled rockets became known to Mr. Tsiolkovsky, if any at all. Certainly, Mr. Tsiolkovsky's research became known to Dr. Goddard even though Dr. Goddard was principally researching rocket engines and fuels. At least three Nations- Russia, Germany, and the United States-benefitted from Mr. Tsiolkovsky's vast research.

CHAPTER 3

Current Space Programs

NASA was established in 1958, succeeding the National Advisory Committee for Aeronautics (NACA). The new agency was to have a distinctly civilian orientation and encourage peaceful applications in space science.

Since its establishment, most US space exploration efforts have been led by NASA, including the Apollo Moon landing missions, the Skylab space station, and, later, the Space Shuttle. NASA, aside Russia, is supporting the International Space Station. It is also overseeing the development of the Orion Multi-Purpose Crew Vehicle, the Space Launch System (SLS) and other Commercial Crew Vehicles (CCV). NASA is also responsible for the Launch Services Program which provides oversight of launch operations and management for uncrewed/crewed NASA, as well as some other parties, launches.

Per Nation, statistics about Space Programs can be presupposed to be exaggerated and flattering. Cooperation between National Space Programs can also be shared unequally.

The following information shows the most active 22 countries currently participating in space programs
as of 2019. The Year Est'd column shows the year that the Space Agency was finally aggregated.

Country	Agency	Budget	Year Est'd
USA	National Aeronautics and Space Administration	$21,500,000,000	1958
China	China National Space Administration	$8,400,000,000	1990
Esa	European Space Agency	$6,406,000,000	1975
Germany	German Aerospace Center	$4,274,000,000	1997
Russia	Russian Federal Space Agency	$3,272,000,000	1992
France	French Space Agency	$2,700,000,000	1961
India	Indian Space Research Organization	$1,425,000,000	1969
Italy	Italian Space Agency	$1,800,000,000	1988
Japan	Japan Aerospace Exploration Agency	$1,699,000,000	2003
South Korea	Korea Aerospace Research Institute	$583,000,000	1989
United Kingdom	UK Space Agency	$500,000,000	2010
Iran	Iranian Space Agency	$393,000,000	2004
Algeria	Algerian Space Agency	$360,000,000	2002
Canada	Canadian Space Agency	$246,000,000	1989
Belgium	Space Agency of Belgium	$224,000,000	1975
Spain	Instituto Nacional de Technica Aeroespacial	$211,000,000	1975
Switzerland	Swiss Space Agency	$177,000,000	1975
Netherlands	Netherlands Space Office	$110,000,000	1975
Sweden	Swedish National Space Agency	$100,000,000	1975
Norway	Norwegian Space Agency	$97,000,000	1987

This list is given of National Space Agencies Program Budgets in ranking order:

Agency	Budget (expressed in millions of US Dollars)
NASA (USA)	21,500
CNSA (China)	8,400
ESA (Europe)	6,406
DLR (Germany)	4,274
Roscosmos (Russia)	3,272
CNES (France)	2,700
ASI (Italy)	1,800
JAXA (Japan)	1,699
ISRO (India)	1,425
KARI (South Korea)	583
UKSA (United Kingdom)	500
ISA (Iran)	393
ASA (Algeria)	360
CSA (Canada)	246
INTA (Spain)	211
SSO (Switzerland)	177
NSO (Netherlands)	110
SNSA (Sweden)	100
NOSA (Norway)	97
SSAU (Ukraine)	80
ALR (Austria)	75
ISA (Israel)	48
AEB (Brazil)	47
CONAE (Argentina)	45

Keep in mind, that this data is the published information of the National agencies and does not include contracted private companies, collateral operations, and similar details. The vagaries of financial reporting are well-known.

The intended purpose of any Space Agency is unknown although it is presumed to be peaceful Space Exploration. Monitoring Space Agencies are not the responsibility of any Agency, including NASA.

CHAPTER 4

Mishaps along the Way

Space Exploration is obviously hazardous! Even though known hazards are mitigated as completely as can be achieved, both known hazards and unknown hazards can occur without notice or even hint of developing.

All of the sacrifices incurred for the advancement of Space Exploration cannot be made complete here, but I can recite the names of the 22 Honorees as listed on the Space Mirror Memorial at the John F. Kennedy Space Center Visitor Complex on Merritt Island, Florida as of 2020.

1. Theodore Freeman died during training on October 31, 1964. He is regarded as being the "First Casualty of the United States Space Program".

2. Elliot See and Charles Bassett died together during training on February 28, 1966.

3. Gus Grissom, Ed White, and Roger Chaffee died together when fire broke out in the Apollo 1 capsule during training on January 27, 1967.

4. Clifton Williams died during training on October 5, 1967.

5. Michael J. Adams died in an X-15 crash on November 15, 1967.

6. Robert H. Lawrence, Jr. died in an F-105 crash on December 8, 1967.

7. Francis Scobee, Michael J. Smith, Ronald McNair, Gregory Jarvis, Judith Resnik, Ellison Onizuka, and Christa McAuliffe all perished during the Challenger disaster on January 28, 1986. McAuliffe is the only civilian listed here.

8. M. L. "Sonny" Carter died while traveling on NASA business on April 5, 1991.

9. Rick Husband, William C. McCool, David M. Brown, Kalpana Chawla, Michael P. Anderson, Laurel Clark, and Ilan Ramon all perished during the Columbia disaster on February 1, 2003.

This summary of Human lives lost during the United States Space Program is given with reverence to those who knew the risks they were taking yet took them anyway for the sake of Space Exploration. In doing so, the inestimable number of those who would follow can do so with as much resolution and heightened confidence.

Space Exploration began in Germany in the 1930's with pre-war experiments of rocket engines. Information is available of lives lost due to rocket engine malfunctions, both historically and by Nation, and is partially given here, summarily:

In the 1930's, ten lives were lost in four separate events, including Max Valier who is regarded as the "First Casualty of the Modern Space Age".

In the 1960's, the" Space Race" was being hotly contested by the United States and the Soviet Union. It caused the worst disaster in the Soviet Union's Space Program-the Nedelin Catastrophe-at the Baikonur Cosmodrome in Kazakhstan. 78 lives were lost in that single instance when an R-16 Rocket second stage exploded on the Launch Pad on October 24, 1960.

Exactly 3 years later at the same Cosmodome, either seven or eight people lost their lives when an R-9 Desna Rocket exploded. This second disaster encouraged the Soviet Union to mark October 24th as a "Black Day" and forbids rocket launches on that day.

On April 14, 1964, the United States suffered three lives lost at Cape Canaveral, Florida when a Delta Rocket caught fire. Static electricity caused ignition of the oxygen rich atmosphere within the capsule.

On May 7, 1964, West Germany suffered three lives lost when a mail rocket exploded at launch.

Overall in the 1960's, five Space Program disasters occurred in three countries with a total loss of approximately 93 lives. That Decade was the deadliest of all Decades in the whole of all Space Programs as of 2020 A.D.

In the 1970's, one Space Program disaster occurred on June 26, 1973 in the Soviet Union when a Kosmos-3M Rocket exploded while launching, nine lives were lost.

In the 1980's, one Space Program disaster occurred on March 18, 1980 in the Soviet Union and it is the second-most fatal disaster of all Space Program disasters. Forty-eight people died during an explosion that happened when a Vostok-2 Rocket was being fueled up at the Plesetsk Cosmodrome.

In the 1990's, five Space Program disasters occurred involving four Nations-the United States, Japan, Sweden, and China. Each country suffered one fatality each, except China.

On January 26, 1995, China lost more than six lives when a Long March 2E Rocket veered off course and crashed. On February 15, 1996, a Long March 3B Rocket also veered off course and crashed into a small village. The death toll of those two Space Program disasters are ambiguous, however they are estimated to be at least twelve fatalities and possibly more than a hundred fatalities. The 1996 Space Program disaster was definitely the more serious of the two disasters.

In the first decade of the 21st Century, three Space Program disasters occurred in three countries-Russia, USA, and Brazil. Brazil suffered the greatest. Twenty-one lives in Brazil were lost on August 22, 2003 when a VLS-1 Rocket exploded while being prepared for launch.

The only failure of a Soyuz-U Rocket happened on October 15, 2002 above the Plesetsk Cosmodrome shortly after Launch. One soldier on the ground was killed.

On July 26, 2007, three civilian contractors were killed in the USA during a rocket engine test. All three were employed by the private firm, Scaled Composites, and represent the first independent casualties of the Space Program. All three are included here because private companies, such as SpaceX, Virgin Galactica, and Blue Origins, are gaining credibility as civilian participants in the Space Program.

Although the accomplishments of all Space Programs are remarkable and many more accomplishments are yet to be discovered, the extremely dangerous nature of Space Exploration is not reflected accurately in the facts given here. The Future belongs to the Brave!

CHAPTER 5

Notable Rockets

_____

The first rockets were powered by solid-fueled propellants (gun powder) in 13th Century China. This type of rocket endured without modification or improvement for several Centuries and eventually made its way West, through India, to Europe.

Although many sizes and designs of solid-fueled rockets existed for many years, the accuracy and range of rockets used for combat was not improved upon until the 19th Century. By the middle of the 19th Century, solid-fueled rockets became a supplement to artillery battalions and were launched in salvos of six or more.

In 1861, rockets were first conceived for a purpose other than war. Sir William Leitch wrote about the prospect of enabling space travel by using rockets then. Nearly fifty years later in 1903, Space Program Founder Konstatin Tsiolkovsky also conceived that idea.

The first liquid-fueled rocket documented to have flown was affectionately named "Nell" by its inventor, Professor Robert H. Goddard. "Nell" was fueled by gasoline and liquid oxygen, never ascended above 100 feet altitude before running out of fuel, but first flew on March 16, 1926.

Professor Goddard built the Goddard 1 through Goddard 4 before starting the A series rockets, then L series rockets. His work was interrupted on the P series rockets by the Second World War. Altogether, there were more than 35 liquid-fueled rockets built.

Professor Goddard's work on the A-4 Rocket was replicated by SS Major Wernher von Braun for purposes of war during the Second World War and the V-2 Rocket began production.

The V-2 Rocket, here on display at Peenemunde, Germany is generally regarded as the predecessor of modern rockets.

After the Second World War, Professor von Braun and 700 other former Nazi Rocket Scientists moved to the United States and started work on the Redstone family of Rockets.

The United States Rocket Program continued within the United States Army Ballistic Missile Agency and developed further with the Atlas family of Rockets.

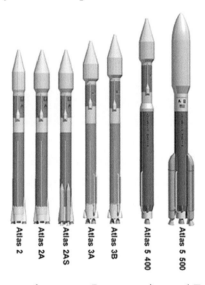

The Atlas Rockets Program began as Intercontinental Ballistic Missiles (ICBM) in the late 1950's and continue today (2020) with the Atlas 5 Series. The Atlas LV-3B Rocket launched four Astronauts into Low Earth Orbit (LEO) as part of Project Mercury.

In 1958, NASA became established and assumed most of the United States' Space Exploration Programs. The Saturn 5 Rocket became their premier rocket certified for crew transport. It was used to put the first two astronauts on the Moon.

15 Saturn 5 Rockets were built between 1967 and 1973, 13 were actually launched as America's only "human-rated super heavy-lift launch vehicles". This new category of Rockets was capable of launching a three-man crew and payload beyond LEO and to Lunar orbit.

As of 2009, the Saturn 5 Rocket holds the record for tallest, heaviest, and most powerful Rocket with 5 Rocketdyne F-1 Rocket engines producing 7,891,000 lbf of thrust with the first stage. The second stage had 5 Rocketdyne J-2 Rocket engines producing 1,155,800 lbf of thrust. The third stage had one Rocketdyne J-2 Rocket engine producing 232,250 lbf of thrust.

The Saturn 5 Rocket Program began in 1960 with Saturn 1 at Marshall Space Flight Center in Huntsville, Alabama. Original plans were for one large Rocket on the first stage, like the V-2 Rocket, but that was quickly dropped. The third and fourth rocket designs (C-3 and C-4) were designed with an Earth Orbit Rendezvous (EOR) maneuver to the Lunar Mission in mind.

The base of the first stage was determined to be strong enough for a fifth F-1 Rocket engine and plans were finalized for the Saturn 5 Rocket to be built. NASA approved the build with a Lunar Orbit Rendezvous (LOR) in 1962 and the Apollo Program was initiated.

The first launch of a Saturn 5 Rocket happened on November 9, 1967 with the Apollo 4 Mission The last launch of a Saturn 5 Rocket happened on May 14, 1973 with the Skylab Mission. After a substantial delay (1981!), the Space Transportation System (STS) then the Space Launch System (SLS) would assume future American Space Exploration duties.

CHAPTER 6

The Space Transportation System (STS)

After the Saturn 5 Rocket was retired on May 13, 1973, the Space Shuttles assumed future missions. Unlike previous spacecraft, the Space Shuttle was reusable and was oftentimes referred to as a "Space Truck".

Space Shuttle Columbia launching from LC 39A at Cape Canaveral, Florida on Space Transportation System 1 (STS-1), April 12, 1981. This is the first launch of the Space Shuttle to orbit. The program would endure for over 30 years until STS-135 on July 8, 2011.

At launch, the Space Shuttle was comprised of four principal components;

1. The Space Shuttle

2. The External Tank

3. Two Solid Rocket Boosters (SRBs)

The Space Shuttles

Six Space Shuttles were built between 1976 and 1992-Enterprise, Columbia, Challenger, Atlantis, Discovery, and Endeavour. All Shuttles are designated as Orbiter Vehicles (OV) in series of manufacture.

Space Shuttle Enterprise OV-101

The Enterprise was built on September 17, 1976 for ALT (Approach and Landing Testing) and was never outfitted with engines or the systems required for space flight though they could've been outfitted at a future time. It was originally to be named the Shuttle Constitution, but President Gerald Ford renamed it the Shuttle Enterprise after a public campaign favored the TV show, Star Trek.

The Shuttle Enterprise was launched from the top of a Boeing 747 modified for such duty: a Shuttle Carrier Aircraft (SCA). The Shuttle was towed from Palmdale, California to Dryden Flight Research Center where it was mounted to the SCA.

Five tests were done without a crew or activation to test flight characteristics of the "lifting body". The Shuttle Enterprise remained mounted to the SCA for the next three tests when astronauts checked out the flight control systems.

On January 12, 1977, the Shuttle Enterprise flew independently under astronaut control. Four more test flights were done with various weights and configurations. The final two tests included three Rocketdyne F-1 Rocket Engines and equipment required for space flight.

After successful testing of Shuttle Enterprise's flight characteristics, it was flown to Marshall Space Flight Center (MSFC) in Huntsville, Alabama aboard the SCA on March 13, 1978. There it was assembled to the External Tank and both Solid Rocket Boosters (SRBs) for the first time to begin Mated Vertical Ground Vibration Tests.

After the entire Shuttle Transportation System (STS) proved it could handle the rigors of the Launch, the Shuttle Enterprise was returned to Palmdale, California for outfitting as a fully operational Space Shuttle. The Shuttle Enterprise entered the Launch Schedule for its maiden flight in July 1981.

Design changes had occurred, especially regarding the weight of fuselage and wings. After reconsiderations of time and costs, the Shuttle Enterprise was retired in favor of completing the Shuttle Columbia. The Shuttle Challenger would take its place.

The Shuttle Enterprise was stripped of many components and sent away as a museum display to the Smithsonian Institution. It assisted in a few post-accident investigations but remains in storage at the National Air and Space Museum at Dulles International Airport in Texas,

Ownership of the Shuttle Enterprise changed from the Smithsonian Institution to the Intrepid Sea, Air, and Space Museum on December 12, 2011 and it has been on public display since July 19, 2012.

Space Shuttle Columbia OV-102

The Shuttle Columbia's maiden flight occurred on April 12, 1981 and it became America's first operational Space Shuttle. It flew 28 STS Missions before it was tragically lost on re-entry on February 1, 2003 with all hands-on board (STS-107). Shuttle Columbia performed flawlessly for over 21 years and completed the first five consecutive STS Missions of America's Space Exploration Program. Shuttle Columbia launched once from White Sands Space Harbor (STS-03), 12 times from Edwards Air Force Base, and the balance from Kennedy Space Center in Florida. The disaster began on Lift-off from Kennedy Space Center when a chilled shard of foam peeled off the External Tank and struck the leading edge of the left wing of the Shuttle. Damage to the wing was unseen and unknown for the duration of the STS-107 Mission (January 16 to February 1, 2003).

The heat shield was damaged. On previous STS Missions and other Shuttles, damage to heat shields had happened before, usually with awareness, and the Mission continued without incident. Insulating foam of the External Tank routinely fell off but never before had it caused any damage.

Although Commander Husband offered to perform an EVA (Extra-Vehicular Activity) and inspect for damage, NASA managers overrode that offer because, even if damage was discovered, there was no known procedure to effect repairs. NASA determined that sustaining the Mission with a possible unknown hazard was acceptable and Commander Husband complied.

The lost crew of STS-107 were (from Left to Right)-

1. **Mission Specialist David M. Brown**

2. **Commander Rick D. Husband**

3. **Mission Specialist Laurel Clark**

4. **Mission Specialist Kalpana Chawla**

5. **Payload Commander Michael P. Anderson**

6. **Pilot William C. McCool**

7. **Payload Specialist Ilan Ramon**

Space Shuttle Challenger OV-099

The history of Space Shuttle Challenger is consumed by its Disaster that happened on January 28, 1986 as it was the first Disaster of the STS program. The Shuttle Challenger was the second operational Shuttle built and deployed 10 satellites on 9 STS Missions starting with STS-06 on April 4, 1983.

The Shuttle Challenger started as a Structural Test Article (STA-099) and when outfitting Shuttle Enterprise appeared to be too difficult, it was decided to make Shuttle Challenger out of STA-099. This method would permit the newer design criteria that occurred.

The Space Shuttler Challenger Disaster was blamed on the right Solid Rocket Booster (SRB) burning through two O-rings at the splice joint, the Booster wall, and impinging on the External Tank wall. The Liquid Hydrogen tank wall within the External Tank became compromised and the entire STS instantly exploded. The two SRBs separated and were directed to collide with each other. The crew capsule also separated and impacted the Atlantic Ocean at more than 200 G's of force and near the shore after the explosion happened 73 seconds after Launch.

No abort procedure could have saved the crew at that point in the Ascent phase. The prospect of an SRB O-ring failure during Launch was calculated, however NASA management overruled lower management concerns of failure and proceeded.

The lost crew of STS-51-L were (from Left to Right)-

1. **Mission Specialist Ellison Onizuka**

2. **Pilot Michael J. Smith**

3. **Space Participant Sharon Christie McAuliffe**

4. **Commander Dick Scobee**

5. **Payload Specialist Gregory Jarvis**

6. **Mission Specialist Ronald McNair**

7. **Mission Specialist Judith Resnik**

An abort procedure was never devised for the STS program. Consequently, STS Launches were never deliberately aborted.

No abort plan existed for the interim before the Shuttle could reach sufficient altitude to initiate a Return to Land (RTL) procedure in which the Shuttle would separate and glide to a landing on a runway or the Atlantic Ocean. Shuttle runways existed in Africa but have never been used.

Space Shuttle Discovery OV-103

The Space Shuttle Discovery served Nasa's STS Program for over 27 years with 39 Missions from STS-41-D on August 30, 1984 through STS-133 on February 24, 2011. Altogether, 252 Astronauts served on STS Discovery Missions.

More notable Discovery Missions include Missions STS-26 on September 29, 1988 which was the first "Return to Flight" after the Shuttle Challenger disaster. STS-114 on July 26, 2005 and STS -121 on July 4, 2006 which were the first "Return to Flight" after the Shuttle Columbia disaster. STS-31 Mission on April 24, 1990 launched the Hubble Space Telescope: STS-82 on February 11, 1997 and STS-103 on December 19, 1999 were maintenance flights for the Hubble Space Telescope.

Discovery Mission STS-95 on October 29,1998 took the oldest Astronaut back to Space; Senator John Glenn was 77 years old, at that time, and is a veteran of both Mercury and STS Missions. Shuttle Discovery was retired after completing STS-133 on February 24, 2011.

The Shuttle Discovery was instrumental in construction of the International Space Station and was the first Shuttle to dock with it. It served flawlessly with no incidents while completing the most Missions (39) of any Shuttle.

The Shuttle Discovery stands on display at the Steven F Undar-Hazy Center in Virginia after becoming de-commissioned on March 9, 2011.

Space Shuttle Atlantis OV-104

The Space Shuttle Atlantis served Nasa's STS Program for over years with 33 Missions from STS-51-J on October 3, 1985 through STS-135 on July 6, 2011. Altogether, 207 Astronauts served on STS Atlantis Missions.

The Space Shuttle Atlantis took nearly half as much time to build as the second Shuttle Columbia and was 3.5 tons lighter than Shuttle Columbia. She underwent two Orbiter Maintenance Down Periods (OMDPs) in which she was updated with better electronics and a power supply that could be shared with the International Space Station.

Oddly and during STS-27 on December2, 1988, the Shuttle Atlantis suffered an identical event as Shuttle Columbia and over 700 heat shield tiles were damaged in critical areas of the right wing. A similar chain of events happened, and NASA Managers encouraged the Shuttle crew to continue the Mission with an unknown potential hazard.

Remarkably, the Shuttle Atlantis survived re-entry, the incident was minimized, and precedences were set that would cause the Columbia Disaster. Since then, changes occurred that would prevent similar dismissals from happening.

The Shuttle Atlantis was de-commissioned after STS-135 on July 6, 2011. That was the final flight of the Space Shuttle Program.

It is now displayed at the Kennedy Space Center Visitor's Complex in Florida.

Space Shuttle Endeavour OV-105

The Space Shuttle Endeavour served Nasa's STS Program for over 19 years with 25 Missions from STS-49 on May 7, 1992 through STS-134 on May 16, 2011. Altogether, 173 Astronauts served on STS Discovery Missions.

The Shuttle Endeavour was the last of five operational Shuttles to be built by Rockwell International Space Transportation Systems in May 1991. Acrimoniously, Rockwell International stated that they made no profit on the Shuttle Endeavour despite its $2.2 billion dollar cost.

Shuttle Endeavour docked once with the Mir Space Station and twelve times with the International Space Station. Its principal Launch Site was Kennedy Space Center Launch Pad 39-A but its first launch was at Edwards AFB Launch Pad 39-B.

The Mir Space Station was scheduled for de-orbiting and the Shuttle Endeavour was used feverishly to finish the construction of the International Space Station. STS-134 was supposed to be the final STS Mission flown by the Shuttle Endeavour but with construction plans being what they are, another Mission was added, and it was flown by the Shuttle Atlantis*.

After STS-134 was flown in May 2011, the Shuttle Endeavour was de-commissioned and flown back to California on the back of the Shuttle Carrier Aircraft. It arrived at Los Angeles International Airport on September 21, 2012 and is displayed at the California Science Center in Exposition Park.

STS Components

The Shuttle External Tank

All components were attached to the External Tank which held the Liquid Hydrogen fuel (LH2) and Liquid Oxygen (LOX) oxidizer. The LOX was kept in the upper tank under the Nose Cone. The LH2 tank took up more than half of the lower External Tank.

The Space Shuttle External Tank measured 153.8 feet long and had a diameter of 27.6 feet. It was covered with foam insulation to minimize ice accumulation. The insulation was painted white on the first two Shuttle Missions but was later dismissed due to weight savings.

LH2 capacity of the External Tank was 234,265# at an elevated pressure of 29.3 psi. The Hydrogen tank is larger because Hydrogen is the lightest element. Liquid Hydrogen has a temperature of -424 degrees Fahrenheit.

LOX capacity of the External Tank was 1,387,457# at an elevated pressure of 22 psi. Liquid Oxygen has a temperature of -300 degrees Fahrenheit.

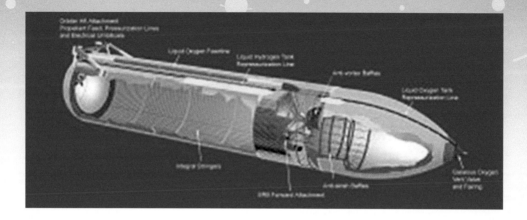

The External Tank delivers both Hydrogen and Oxygen to the Space Shuttle's 3 RS-25 Rocket Motors and remains connected to it until 10 seconds after Main Engines Cut-Off (MECO). At that time, the Space Shuttle is securely aligned with its desired orbit path and becomes detached from the External Tank.

The External Tank is then de-orbited, and it crashes into the Indian Ocean, or the Southern Pacific Ocean, where it remains abandoned. All External Tanks were exploded during re-entry and sank after one mission.

Although plans were developed to use the empty External Tank as a future Space Habitat and kept in LEO, none of these plans were allowed to happen. Concerns about Space Debris and the expenses involved with an improvised Space Station encouraged deorbiting and destroying the once-used External Tank.

The Shuttle Solid Rocket Boosters (SRBs)

The Solid Rocket Boosters (SRBs) were intended for reuse and were recovered after their use as supplemental rockets to the Space Shuttle Missions. The SRBs used solid rocket propellant and were controllable by the thrust vector control system operating the rocket nozzle.

Both of the SRBs provided over 70% of the thrust needed for a successful launch and ascent to around 220,000 feet. The solid propellant precluded any throttling of the SRB, but they could be released from the STS in an emergency situation.

Each SRB weighed 150,000 pounds, stood nearly 150 feet tall, and had a diameter of about 12 feet. Each SRB consists of seven segments spliced together with clevises and pins then sealed with O-rings and paste.

At launch, each SRB weighed 1,260,000 pounds and produced 2,800,000 pound-force (lbf) of thrust. The ½" thick steel walls of the SRB are heavy but an O-ring failure at a splice joint was found to be the defect that caused the first major disaster in NASA's history-the Challenger Disaster.

SRBs are secured to the Mobile Launch Platform by eight hold down bolts and nuts-four per SRB. The Launch Command, in concert with all other commands necessary for Launch, detonates the hold down nuts and releases the complete STS from its hold down posts 126 seconds after Launch, explosive fasteners explode and release both SRBs from the External Tank. Small rockets near the nose of the SRB fire and push the SRBs safely away from the Space Shuttle and External Tank. Each SRBs then descend and parachutes are deployed for a relatively soft, vertical landing in the Atlantic Ocean for recovery.

The SRBs used on STSs were essentially unmodified throughout the Space Shuttle missions and were the largest and most powerful booster rockets ever used of all Space Exploration. Of the 270 SRBs used throughout the STS Program, 264 SRBs were recovered for reuse.

Modifications made after the Challenger Disaster resulted in the Advanced Solid Rocket Booster Program (ASRBP) and a third O-ring being added to the splice joints. Additionally, all SRBs were modified with tougher attachment points to the External Tank and became known as RSRBs (Redesigned Solid Rocket Boosters).

CHAPTER 7

The Super Heavy-Lift Launch Vehicles

Sometime after 1973 and the retirement of Saturn 5, rockets were reidentified as "Super Heavy Lift Launch Vehicles"-SHLLV. This designator includes all the components to the core rocket, the payload, and collateral systems attached at Launch.

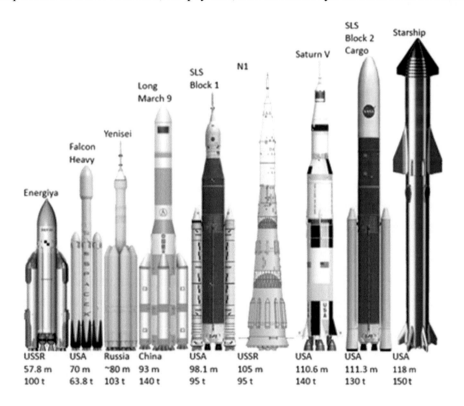

Energiya	Falcon Heavy	Yenisei	Long March 9	SLS Block 1	N1	Saturn V	SLS Block 2 Cargo	Starship
USSR	USA	Russia	China	USA	USSR	USA	USA	USA
57.8 m	70 m	~80 m	93 m	98.1 m	105 m	110.6 m	111.3 m	118 m
100 t	63.8 t	103 t	140 t	95 t	95 t	140 t	130 t	150 t

Nine Super Heavy Lift Rockets exist as of 2020; Five American, three Russian, and one Chinese. Rocket launches are still very expensive, so increased payloads and the required thrust to launch the payload are the preferred tactic for containing costs. Propellant weight has always been the necessary detriment of all rockets.

SHLLVs are described briefly as follows:

1. The Energia SHLLV is a Russian design resembling the Space Shuttle. It was saddled by the Buran spacecraft which operated similar to the Space Shuttle. The first Energia SHLLV launched on May 15, 1987 but failed to enter LEO and it landed prematurely. The second Energia SHLLV launched on November 15, 1988 and the Buran spacecraft orbited the Earth twice before landing in Russia. Thereafter, the Energia Program was cancelled because of social problems not related to the Space Program.

2. The Falcon Heavy SHLLV is an American design contracted by NASA with a private company, SpaceX. It combines the three rockets of the Falcon 9 Model into the Falcon Heavy SHLLV and has delivered Elon Musk's Tesla Roadster Car into a heliocentric orbit. Production continues with the Falcon Heavy 5B SHLLV.

3. Yenisei (Irtysh or Soyuz-5) is a Russian design that is proposed to be developed in 2022 as a replacement for the Angares and Zenit Rockets.

4. Long March-9 SHLLV is a Chinese design/improvement of the Long March family of rockets and is, by far!, huge with a Lift off Mass of 3,000 tons and height of between 305 and 360 feet. No date for the Maiden Flight of Long March 9 SHLLV or Long March 11 SHLLV is known.

5. SLS Block 1 SHLLV is built for Nasa's Artemis Program and for the Lunar Gateway . It is built by United Launch Alliance. It is proposed to launch in 2022 or 2023.

6. The N1 SHLLV is a Russian design that failed to reach orbit four times. It was suspected that the 30 NK-15 Rocket engines could not stabilize in the Launch Trajectory and the NI SHLLV was cancelled.

7. The Saturn 5 Rocket was retired in 1973 before SHLLVs were designated but is included here.

8. The SLS Block 2 Cargo SHLLV is NASA's collaboration with Boeing and NG Innovations to launch 130,000 pounds to LEO sometime in the late 2020's.

9. The Starship SHLLV is NASA's contract with SpaceX due to launch in 2020. It is the only SHLLV that has the Starship integrated on the nose of the first stage and offers reusability through VTVL Technology. It proposes more than 100,000 pounds of Maximum Take-off Mass and future use as the first Spacecraft to Mars.

The SHLLV programs of launching 50,000 pounds or more of Total Launch Mass have proven to be near the extreme limit of what is possible. Attaining the Escape Velocity required to reach LEO with such weight is truly difficult! The historically few successful SHLLV launches could be improved upon by discovering new technologies, lessening loads, or some other rectifying thought but, as things stand today, the only working plan is to keep trying what we're presently doing with hopes of someday finding a better way.

Historically, rockets have progressed predictably to the standards established by the Saturn 5 rocket in the 1960's-payloads of more than 100,000 pounds delivered to LEO. Extant current missions of servicing the International Space Station and constructing communication networks in Earth Orbit could have been accomplished by the Saturn 5 rocket without further rocket development over the past sixty years. However, the Saturn 5 rocket and its systems became obsoleted on May 14, 1973 with the advancement of the STS system.

The STS system and its five Orbiting Vehicles assumed all NASA missions beginning on April 12, 1981 when OV-101, Space Shuttle Columbia, made its maiden flight. The STS system is responsible for the construction of the International Space Station and numerous other missions, including launching and fixing the Hubble Space Telescope. After 135 missions and 30 years of STS operations, OV-105, Space Shuttle Atlantis made the final landing of the Space Transportation System on July 6, 2011.

After the STS, servicing the International Space Station became the responsibility of the Russian Space Agency, Roscosmos, because NASA had no SHLLV rocket capable of the task. Roscosmos performed flawlessly for more than ten years before recent competition for NASA contracts to service the ISS were awarded to Boeing and SpaceX. SpaceX developed a SHLLV rocket called the Falcon Heavy while Boeing depends on United Launch Alliance (ULA) to build the Atlas 5 rocket that launches their CST-100 Starliner Capsule. Blue Origin is also developing a SHLLV rocket-the New Glenn.

SHLLVs are supposedly the best method for Space Exploration despite their adherence to first principles used in the original rockets a Century ago. Concepts, such as VTVL, angular momentum, asymmetrical thrust, and many others, have only recently been experimented with. The ultimate rocket might not resemble Professor Goddard's A-4 rocket.

CHAPTER 8

The Space Launch System (SLS)

After the Space Transportation System ended and the last Shuttle Atlantis landed on July 21, 2011, NASA had continuation plans already drafted to tend to the International Space Station, to redirect asteroids for prevention of a collision with Earth (Asteroid Redirect Maneuver or ARM), to enhance communication satellites, and to improve space science projects. The new program would be without Shuttles and would be called The Artemis Program, named after the Greek twin sister of Apollo and Goddess of the Moon.

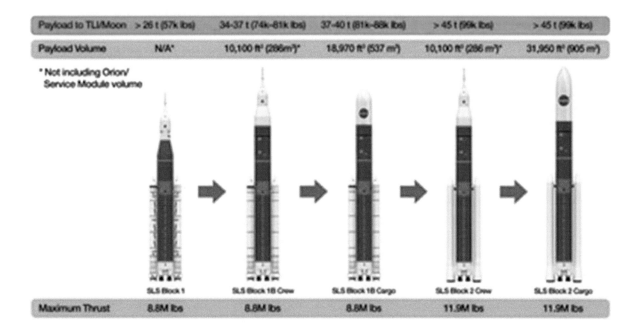

Payload to TLI/Moon	> 26 t (57k lbs)	34-37 t (74k–81k lbs)	37-40 t (81k–88k lbs)	> 45 t (99k lbs)	> 45 t (99k lbs)
Payload Volume	N/A*	10,100 ft² (286m³)*	18,970 ft² (537 m³)	10,100 ft² (286 m³)*	31,950 ft² (905 m³)

* Not including Orion/ Service Module volume

	SLS Block 1	SLS Block 1B Crew	SLS Block 1B Cargo	SLS Block 2 Crew	SLS Block 2 Cargo
Maximum Thrust	8.8M lbs	8.8M lbs	8.8M lbs	11.9M lbs	11.9M lbs

The Ares family of SHLLVs are to be NASA's substitution for the STS Program anf the start of the LOP-G missions (Lunar Orbital Program-Gateway).

The Artemis Program, as the initial program to advance the LOP-G program, has been hampered by lack of funding by the U.S. Congress but has been sustained by funds derived from international sources, the U.S. Air Force, reconnaissance agencies, and the like.

NASA's federal budget, et al, is less than half of 1% of the total Federal Budget and is barely sufficient to maintain the U.S. Space Exploration program as it was originally intended. NASA is also involved in many other space-related programs, other than rocket science, that incur additional costs upon NASA's already frail budget. Consequently, deadlines are delayed.

In the case of the Artemis and the LOP-G programs, it has been nine years since the end of the STS program (2011) and the proposed first launch of the Artemis Program (2020). Although there have been a few tests in preparation for the Artemis Program, a firm agenda for the Artemis Program is still not proposed-such is the common uncertainty inherent to Space Exploration. Future dates for mission accomplishments are given but it is generally understood that they are indefinite.

The Artemis Program is divided into 7 phases as of 2020. Artemis 1, 2, and 3 are expected to be launched by the SLS Block 1 SHLLV. U.S. Congress mandated that the first block of SHLLVs be capable of launching 209,000# to LEO. Block 1B SHLLVs are intended to launch the Exploratory Upper Stage and begin Artemis Programs 4, 5, 6, and 7. Block 2 SHLLVs are intended to launch 330,000# to LEO, launch the Orion Spacecraft, and enable the first Human flights to Mars. Any failure of any Artemis Program or Block of SHLLVs is fully expected to delay future Artemis Program.

The Lunar Orbital Program-Gateway program (LOP-G) actually is two separate programs combined. Both have goals toward colonization of the Mars planet.

The Lunar Orbital Program (LOP) is to establish a Space Station in orbit around the Moon and also Lunar Surface Assets. Essentially, LOP is to facilitate colonization of the Moon.

The Gateway Program (G) is to establish a "Gateway" to facilitate "Deep Space" explorations, either with or without assistance from the LOP program.

Artemis 3 is planned to be the first crewed visit to the Lunar Surface since the Apollo 17 mission in 1972. Artemis 1 and 2 missions will preposition logistical support for the Artemis 3 mission. Artemis 3 is proposed for the year 2024, Subsequent Artemis missions are proposed to happen each year thereafter until Artemis 7 in the year 2028.

The complexities of planning future Space Programs are fluidic and subject to change without notice.

CHAPTER 9

Space Stations

Space Stations are not a new idea. They were first illustrated in schoolbooks in the 1960's after being first drawn by Professor Wernher von Braun in 1952. Almost all Space Stations were of "rotating wheel" construction because artificial gravity was known, even back then, to be essential for Human habitat.

The concept of Space Stations actually started a hundred years previous to that; well before even rockets became known. The credit for the first mention of the invention of a Space Station is given to writer Edward Everett Hale for his work in his 1869 book, "The Brick Moon".

It is not known if "The Brick Moon" was ever read by Space Program Founder Konstatin Tsiolkovsky or if it was another one of his many brilliant ideas, however Mr. Tsiolkovsky understood the important functions that could be accomplished with assistance from a manned Space Station. Such talk in those days probably was generally regarded as foolishness.

Within two decades, near the start of the 20th Century, a second Space Program Founder, Professor Julius Oberth, realized the functionality of Space Stations. Still without rockets to reach them, he knew that his futuristic thoughts would be mostly for his personal musings.

In 1929, a Slovene writer named Herman Potocnik published, "The Problem of Space Travel" and it made first mention of a "rotating wheel" to produce artificial gravity. Nearly a century later, such a notion has never been built!

Space Stations are of two types of construction-monolithic (one-piece) or modular with modular being the preferred method of construction because large volumes and heavy weights are difficult to launch. Similarly, modular construction involves construction in Space: an equally difficult endeavor.

After permanent construction of modules, Space Stations are referred to as monolithic construction and they are de-orbited as one piece at the end of their service life. Replacement of old modules with modern modules can extend the service life of a Space Station

Only Soviet monolithic Space Stations meant for civilian exploratory missions originally existed starting on April 19, 1971 with the Salyut 1 Space Station. It was quickly followed by the American Space Station "Skylab"-1973 through 1979. Both of these Space Station had only one docking position and stays on-board were usually limited to 90 days.

These first two Space Stations were of limited capabilities and, although a few Space experiments were tried, they resembled earlier Spacecraft and rockets. The higher radiation and lack of gravity while on board a Space Station had unknown effects on the Human body at that time, so safety concerns dictated short stays on-board the Space Station.

As of 2020, the duration record for continuous time in Space was set by Soviet Cosmonaut Valeri Polyakov at 437.75 days in 1995. Several other astronauts have endured time in Space for approximately a year, or so, but Space effects on Human health are sometimes severe! Eventually, blood vessels begin to hemorrhage and radiation outside Earth's Magnetosphere can cause afflictions only recently discoverable.

Monolithic Space Stations served from 1971 through 1986. They were typically of Soviet construction and required frequent crew rotations. The United States cooperated with the Soviet Union to assure a successful transition to the current International Space Station in 1998.

The Chinese have cancelled plans for their Space Station Program Tiangong-3 in 2003.

Chinese secrecy is probably the reason little is known about their Space Exploration plans. Presently, they continue independently and without assistance from any other National Space Program.

The entire brief history of Russian and American manned Space Stations is listed here;

1. Salyut 1, 19 April 1971-11 October 1971.

2. DOS-2, 29 July1972, failed during launch.

3. Salyut 2, 4 April 1973-28 May 1973

4. Kosmos 557, 11 May 1973-22 May 1973, failed during orbit.

5. Skylab, 14 May 1973-11 July 1979.

6. Salyut 3, 25 June 1974-24 January 1975

7. Salyut 4, 26 December 1974-3 February 1977.

8. Salyut 5, 22 June 1976-8 August 1977

9. Salyut 6, 29 September 1977-29 July 1982

10. Salyut 7, 19 April 1982-7 February 1991

11. Mir, 19 February 1986-23 March 2001

12. ISS 12 July 2000-proposed for end of service in 2028.

The Chinese Space Program joined this international endeavor when they launched their Tiangong Space Station Program in September 2011. Tiangong translates to "Heavenly Palace" in English.

Tiangong-1 overlapped with Tiangong-2 for a couple of years before being de-orbited on April 2, 2018. Tiangong-2 was also de-orbited on July 19, 2019 after three years of service.

The Chinese manned Space Stations were Tiangong 1 and Tiangong 2. Tiangong 1 was launched on 29 September 2011 and de-orbited on 2 April 2018. Tiangong 2 was launched on 15 September 2016 and de-orbited on 19 July 2019.

Tiangong 3 has been cancelled and no future Chinese Space Stations are planned though China continues a Chinese Lunar Exploration Program (CLEP) with the Chang'e missions of autonomous Lunar orbiters and Lunar rovers. Chang'e is the name of the Chinese Moon goddess.

Since April 2011, the People's Republic of China has been banned from NASA associations and visits to the International Space Station because of suspicions of Chinese spying on our technology. This level of distrust happens in both directions.

Since November 2017, China and Russia have entered into a cooperative agreement to further Space Exploration. Such cooperation might assist in China's goal of landing a crewed mission on the Moon. Apparently, spying and patent rights are of lesser consternation between communist nations.

Revolving Space Stations have been designed for the past 75 years or longer but as of 2020, none have been built to use artificial gravity. The cost, weight and volume are considered too large. Current purposes are being met by one singular International Space Station.

CHAPTER 10

The Game Changers

Game Changers, in this context, are individuals who independently asserted themselves into National Space Programs and constructed private Space Programs of their own that compliments their National Space Program. This singular sentence explanation cannot accurately define all the traits of a "game changer", even in this context, but it is given here to delineate private individuals from the Nationalistic aspects of all Space Programs.

Many, perhaps the majority of, advantages of private space programs have not been realized because the first privately held space program was founded in 2000-Blue Origin in Kent, Washington. Blue Origin's intent was to enable civilian Human flight into Outer Space by lowering the cost of launching.

Suddenly, two more privately held space programs, SpaceX in 2002 and Virgin Galactic in 2004, became founded in America. A few other privately held space programs became founded in other Countries at about that time.

Blue Origin

Mr. Jeff Bezos founded Blue Origin with revenues that he gained from his sale of Amazon stock. His personal fortune, plus smaller contracts, has sustained Blue Origin's operations from its start in September 2000 through present.

Mr. Bezos has had a curiosity about Space Exploration since a young age which he revealed in his High School valedictorian speech in 1982. 17 years later in 1999, the movie October Sky was released, and it prompted Mr. Bezos to seriously consider building a space company. He discussed the idea with Neal Stephenson, a science fiction writer, and founded Blue Origin the next year.

Mr. Bezos is a very wealthy man with his ownership of Amazon.com With funds from his base enterprise, Blue Origin grew rapidly, had many successes, and employed over 2,000 employees by 2019. Developments in progress promise further growth.

Blue Origin uses names of astronomy pioneers to title their projects and has a company motto of "Grabatim Ferociter" which is Latin for "Step by Step Ferociously". Even the company name is derived from Carl Sagan's referral to Earth being a "pale blue dot" in the vastness of Space.

Mr. Bezos kept his activities relatively secret. His development of his first rocket, the New Shepherd, became somewhat public when he began buying land in Culberson Country, Texas for testing of hardware. The company program of "self-imposed silence" was kept until 2015. Despite this, Blue Origin maintains a discrete exposure to publicity.

Blue Origin launched its first testbed, named Charon, on March 5, 2005. It reached an altitude of 315 feet and tested propulsive landing-Vertical Take-off and Vertical Landing (VTVL). After one flight of Charon, future flights were done with the testbed named Goddard.

Blue Origin developed their rocket engines with the direction of President Rob Meyerson who is presently Senior Vice President of Advance Development Program within Blue Origin. Rocket engines started sequentially with BE-1, the prefix stands for "Blue Engine". Engine development continues beyond BE-7 which is intended to softly land the Blue Moon Lander on the Lunar surface.

BE-1 was the first rocket engine developed by Blue Origin and used on the Goddard testbed, as well as static testing. It produced 2,200 lbf of thrust using HTP (High Test Peroxide) only as a monopropellant system.

BE-2 used a pump-fed bipropellant engine burning kerosene and HTP. This arrangement resembled a modern iteration of what Dr. Goddard used to power his earliest rockets nearly a hundred years earlier. Five BE-2 engines were built and tested on the Propulsive Module (PM-2) testbed in 2011. They produced 31,000 lbf of thrust.

BE-1 and BE-2 tested well and development of BE-3 engine was announced in January 2013. Design criteria was drafted to use Liquid Oxygen and Liquid Hydrogen (LOX/LH2) for a bipropellant system capable of 110,000 lbf of thrust to reach suborbital altitude.

BE-3 engine tests included tests of a precision throttle that would permit Vertical Landings, a relighting system that permitted both engine shutdown and restart, and a Thrust Vector Control System (TVCS) that steered the rocket towards Vertical Landing in reverse flight. Blue Origin's intention of reusability of both rockets and capsules to lessen the expenses of spaceflight was always a principal consideration.

The BE-3 engine was further developed with a nozzle that improved efficiency in the vacuum of Space and was fitted to the capsule which was the second stage. This improved engine is known as the BE-3U and is expendable as the rocket engine must be discarded to facilitate a parachute landing of the New Shepherd capsule. The BE-3 and BE-3U passed acceptance testing in April 2015.

The BE-4 rocket engine development program began in 2011 and was Blue Origin's first rocket to burn LOX and methanol. This type of fuel usage is predicted to allow in situ production of fuels from resources available on lands other than Earth-the Moon, Mars, etc. Establishment of fuel manufacturing facilities on the Moon and other satellites is a key component for expanded Deep Space explorations.

The BE-4 rocket engine is much larger than any of the other Blue Origin engines with 550,000 lbf of thrust. It was not announced publicly until September 2014 about the same time when Blue Origin collaborated with United Launch Alliance (ULA) to co-develop this engine.

ULA and Blue Origin plan to replace an RD-180 Russian rocket with the BE-4 rocket on an upgraded Atlas V launch vehicle. BE-4 testing was expected to be complete by late 2018. The Atlas V launch vehicle will be succeeded by the Vulcan SHLLV with 2 BE-4 rocket engines.

The BE-4 rocket engine is also being sought for use on Boeing's spaceplane-DARPA XS-1, Orbital ATK launch vehicles, commercial sales, and, of course, Blue Origin's New Glenn orbital launch vehicle. The BE-4 rocket engine has market competition from SpaceX Raptor engine and various foreign manufacturers.

The BE-7 rocket engine is smaller at 10,000 lbf of thrust but is mission-specific to the Blue Moon Lander. The Lander requires precise throttle control of the BE-7 for descent to the Lunar surface. Additional thrust is not required where gravity is $1/6^{th}$ that of Earth.

Blue Origin also partnered with Aerojet Rocketdyne to develop a pusher launch escape using solid rocket motors and thrust vector control systems. Although it is not throttleable, it does allow steering for a safe egress from a launch abort procedure.

The New Shepherd Rocket, named after Astronaut Alan Shepherd, was Blue Origin's first rocket propelled by its BE-3 rocket engine. It perfected VTVL and proved reusability of rockets could reduce expenses. Its maiden flight happened on April 29, 2015.

New Shepherd proved what Mr. Bezos intended from start. - "lower the cost of spaceflight so that…we humans can better continue exploring the solar system." His second objective for Blue Origin was "to increase the safety of human spaceflight."

The New Glenn SHLLV is named after Astronaut John Glenn and its first stage will be powered by seven BE-4 engines. It is huge and is still in development after being announced in September 2016. No date is estimated for its maiden flight.

The next project after New Glenn is New Armstrong, named after Astronaut Neil Armstrong. Although not much else is known about New Armstrong, other than its name, the fact that future plans are made by Blue Origin to ferociously aggress a firm agenda of Space Exploration.

Blue Origin continues, step by step, with private funding of about a billion dollars per year provided by Mr. Bezos plus contract payments from collaborations with NASA. The future sounds certain for the progress made by Blue Origin.

SpaceX

SpaceX is an abbreviation of "Space Exploration Technology Corporation". It was founded in Hawthorne, California in 2002 by Sir Elon Musk, FSA, with the mission of colonizing Mars and making humans a "multi-planetary species". It intends to accomplish this by reducing space transportation costs; principally, by the "rapid reusability" of rockets and capsules and vertical integration of manufacturing "in-house". These two advantages and other advantages have enabled SpaceX to decrease launch costs by well over half that of competitor's costs!

Elon Musk attempted to purchase an ICBM rocket from Russia after not being able to locate an affordable rocket in America. He was rebuked in Russia and returned home with a firm plan to build his own rocket from scratch. His estimation of costs predicted that SpaceX could produce a rocket many times more efficiently. He was correct.

By assembling an excellent team of engineers under the supervision of Mr. Tom Mueller and using vertical integration processes, Elon Musk began building the Falcon family of rockets starting with the Falcon 1.

The Falcon 1 Rocket is propelled by a single Merlin 1A rocket engine on the first stage and a Kestrel engine on the second stage. Both engines used LOX/RP-1, an oxygen and kerosene blend, but the Kestrel engine ran off tank pressure after the Merlin engine was fed by a turbopump.

Five flights of the Falcon 1 rocket occurred between March 24, 2006 and July 14, 2009. The first three are listed as failures for various reasons. The fourth launch on September 28, 2008 was a success and marked SpaceX as the first privately funded space company to secure a satellite in a LEO. The fifth flight on July 14, 2009 was also a success but was the final flight of the Falcon 1 rockets before being succeeded by the Falcon 9 rocket.

Falcon 9 version 1 flew from 2010-2013. Falcon 9 v1.1 flew from 2013-2016. The present version, Falcon 9 v1.2, is Block 5 Full Thrust version of SpaceX's EELV (Evolved Expendable Launch Vehicle). The Falcon 9 rocket qualified for the National Security Launch Program and secured NASA contracts for COTS (Commercial Orbital Transportation Services) services to the International Space Station.

The Falcon 9 v1.2 failed to vertically land on an Autonomous Spaceport Drone Ship (ASDS) named "Of Course I Still Love You" three times. This critical tactic to secure the first stage for "rapid reusability" became doubted and future flights were in jeopardy of losing this recovery tactic to lessen launch costs.

On the fourth attempt completed in January 2015, hydraulic pressure was lost to the grid fins used for steering and the rocket was damaged on impact with the ASDS.

On the fifth attempt completed in April 2015, a bipropellant valve became stuck shortly after launch. This rocket was also lost on impact with the ASDS.

The first successful VTVL procedure on an ASDS occurred in April 2016. Of the 16 tests of VTVL done between 2013 and 2016, on both land and sea, six Falcon 9 rockets were recovered for reuse on future missions.

The next development was for the Falcon Heavy SHLLV. It was announced in 2011 with a proposed first flight in 2013. The concept was simple- attach 2 Falcon 9 rockets to a core Falcon 9 rocket for a total of 27 Merlin 1D rocket nozzles- but the execution proved difficult. Five years passed before the maiden flight of Falcon Heavy on February 6, 2018.

The Falcon Heavy SHLLV has little competition. Its total thrust of 3,400,000 lbf produced by the two boosters plus the 1,700,00 lbf produced by the core first stage rocket equals 5,100,000 lbf available total thrust at launch.

The qualifier for an SHLLV is its ability to launch 110,000 pounds (or more) of payload into LEO. These are the largest and most powerful rockets ever built by anyone!

Operational and comparable SHLLVs are the Delta 4 (American), The Long March 5 (Chinese), the Soyuz-5 (Russian), and the Vulcan rocket (American). Several other SHLLVs have tried and failed or just became retired, such as the Saturn 5 rocket.

The quest for larger rockets to further Space Exploration is ongoing.

Proposed SpaceX projects

Sir Musk has proposed the "Big Falcon Rocket", a.k.a. "BFR", in September 2017 at the 68th meeting of the International Astronomical Congress. He detailed plans to build a SHLLV larger than anything built previously and propel it with SpaceX's Raptor engines fueled with methalox fuel-a blend of liquid methane combined with liquid oxygen.

His plans are bold and intriguing!

His original plans for colonizing Mars, first stated in 2001 with the Mars Oasis concept, are in keeping with the development of the BFR but certain processes and procedures must be prepositioned before Man's first interstellar travel. Newly realized opportunities are constantly modifying the original plans of SpaceX.

One of the first actions was to change the name of the original plan from MCT for Mars Colonial Transport to ITS for Interplanetary Transport System because the plans have changed to beyond only Mars travel. Timid limits are being challenged with early successes in what might be called a "second effort" of Space Exploration.

Even the BFR required a name change to "Starship". The Starship retains some of its original features, but canard wings and aerodynamic enhancements make it remarkably improved. Its possible 41 Raptor engines can be turned on or off individually which increases its capabilities well past any previous rocket.

SpaceX has plans to utilize the Starship to provide commercial travel between cities at great distances in record time. For instance, in May 2019, they proposed Starship travel at Mach 20 between Los Angeles, California and New York, New York in 25 minutes. Presently, they're proposing using the Starship to provide space tourism around the Moon and have already booked their first manifest.

Not all future plans of SpaceX are known or could be imagined, however Starlink is one example of the vertical integration that Sir Musk

uses in his development of strategies. Unforeseen hardships that dismantle many other corporations are less likely to happen to SpaceX.

Virgin Galactic

Sir Richard Branson owns over 400 companies and started Virgin Galactic as a space tourism business. As a pioneer of such a business, he used his highly entrepreneurial spirit to investigate a possible business plan and begin development of a program that would enable average citizens to fly above the Karman Line.

The Karman Line is a distinct altitude of 100 kilometers (or 62 miles) above ground level (AGL). Anyone who flies above the Karman Line, with or without the space gear required for sustained exposure to Outer Space, qualifies as an "Astronaut" and receives their Astronaut "wings".

Of course, "Astronaut" is a highly generalized term and it has no or very little qualifying purpose on the bearer of that term. Agencies determine if an astronaut is fit for the specific mission or function planned.

Astronauts are volunteers and can decline any mission or function for any reason without shame or embarrassment. Participants of Virgin Galactic are sure to know that they are "space tourists" and not true "astronauts".

Sir Branson's vision for Virgin Galactic is to make a profit by selling tickets to any interested individual that can afford it. The passenger of a Virgin Galactic flight would board the VSS (Virgin Space Ship) Spaceplane, be air-launched from the Mothership-WhiteKnightTwo, fly above the Karman Line and experience zero gravity, before returning to the Mojave Spaceport. Such a flight is expected to last about an hour.

Before the first flight, tickets are estimated to cost $250,000 and the rigors of rocket flight are expected to be well within the coping abilities of the average person. First flights have been set back since April 2011.

Virgin Galactic suffered a fatal tragedy on October 31, 2014 after VSS Enterprise disintegrated in flight. The ensuing investigation concluded that the feathering system used for the descent stage became unlocked prematurely. About 60-90 seconds after ignition of the rocket engine and while supersonic, the Spaceplane developed aerodynamic instability which caused the aft section of the Spaceplane to come apart. The co-pilot, Mr. Michael Asbury, was killed but the pilot, Mr. Peter Siebold, was able to parachute to safety yet he still suffered severe injuries.

This picture shows the VSS Spaceplane secured to the middle wing of the Mothership-White Knight Two-and prepared for an "air-launch."

In 2015, Virgin Galactic endured criticism from both customers and the media. The accident and an attempt to change from a plasticized fuel to a rubberized fuel for the Spaceplane's rocket engine had caused impatience with the Virgin Galactic space program.

In response, Virgin Galactic developed the LauncherOne, a suborbital launch vehicle originally proposed in 2011. LauncherOne is substantially larger to accommodate orbital insertion of small satellites because the market for space tourism had dwindled somewhat. The engine was also improved from solid-fueled single-stage to liquid-fueled two-stage engines using LOX/RP-1.

The first stage of the Launcher One will be powered by the Newton 3 engine that produces somewhere between 58,000 lbf and 75,000 lbf of thrust after the air launch procedure. Flight will continue after exhaustion of the first stage with a Newton 1 engine that produces about 3,500 lbf of thrust.

After both stages are spent, LauncherOne will glide and return to a landing, presumably at the Mojave Spaceport. The limitations of LauncherOne preclude its use as a commercial transportation system because unpowered landings are typically not allowed at airports.

LauncherOne required a larger Mothership than White Knight Two so a Boeing 747-400 named "Cosmic Girl" was proposed to be fitted with the attachment points for LauncherOne. The Jumbo Jet could reach the air launch altitude of 45,000 feet AGL but a dedicated aircraft capable of higher altitudes was desired.

On October 4, 2004, Mr. Paul Allen, the co-founder of Microsoft, confirmed that he was the sole investor to Scaled Composites which developed the SpaceShipOne. SpaceShip One ascended to a height of 377,591 feet AGL and won the Ansari X Prize of $10,000,000 for being the first private company to put a civilian in Space.

On December 13, 2011, Mr. Allen announced the Stratolaunch System Corporation at Mojave Air and Space Port. He partnered with Orbital ATK and Scaled Composites to build and fly the Stratolauncher as shown. Its maiden flight occurred on April 13, 2019.

Sadly, Stratolaunch System Corporation ceased operations the following month. Air launch procedures were abandoned in favor of the VTVL procedure used by competitors SpaceX and Blue Origin. The space tourism industry as conceived by Virgin Galactic never became profitable and its future is dubious.

Mr. Allen passed away on October 15, 2018. His remarkable life of curiosity and accomplishments is best shown through his philanthropic endeavors. His love of aviation enhanced his productive Life of 65 years duration.

**The Stratolauncher was proven in flight one month before being retired.
The promise of the Air Launch Procedure is still viable.**

CHAPTER 11

The Future of American Space Programs

The future of American Space Programs has been constructed with the Artemis Program by Nasa which has since been delayed and plans to colonize Mars by both SpaceX and Blue Origins which remain, presently, in the planning stages. All Space Programs will forever be seen as ambitious and daunting, however, now that Space Exploration has become a fixture of Modern Life it cannot be made deniable.

It is an integrated component of discussions of Space Programs to aspire beyond each successful rocket launch and imagine what might yet be possible. Although Space Programs have no other reason for existence than human inquisitiveness, the goals attained by such programs have recompensed the customer by an order of magnitude and instilled a level of optimism that is not commonly available through any other human endeavor.

The future of the American Space Program could be reinforced militarily by actions of the United States Space Force (USSF). Perhaps a resurgent social enlightenment for Space Exploration will develop, once again, to protect the Earth from a disastrous collision with an asteroid or some other significant celestial event.

The technological capabilities of Space Programs as they stand today yearn to be used. More receptive collaborations with foreign governments would expand productivity of Space Programs far beyond the passively accepted level of productivity that appeases most everyone today.

Another hindrance to the advancement of sciences, particularly Space Exploration, is the absence of a dedicated monetary fund-very few nations donate willingly to any cause even though they benefit from it. Such a thought is proven to be unwelcome by The United Nation's resistance to it over the past 75 years. It would seem ridiculous if it were not standard practice.

Of course, the global pandemic of coronavirus would be an apt case in point. No Nation should be distressed when relief is possible just on the other side of some border or from a central fund. The collaborations proven by many Space Programs are relatable, with modifications, domestically.

Russia had the lead position of Space Exploration nearly fifty years ago and is still a capable partner to the United States in all matters that deal with the International Space Station. Numerous nations contribute to the International Space Station but with its planned decommissioning happening in 2028 after 30 years of service, plans for future space stations are not forthcoming from any nation other than NASA's LOP/G program.

China's Tiandong-3 space station might become established in five years, but China hasn't made any International offers of cooperation for its use, so far as anyone knows. Collaboration is needed here but the threat of espionage of missile technology is a real hazard.

In light of current world affairs, space programs are at risk and always have been. The business ventures made possible by Space Exploration promise high yields and improvements in our livelihood. Very few people can accurately guess at what limit Space Exploration will take us.

We have accepted current rocket design as practical, so it has stagnated at a level similar to the Saturn 5 Rocket (1973). Since then, fuel and drive improvements have been relegated as unnecessary. Rocket capacity matching the Saturn 5's performance is still a difficult achievement.

Complication of any system is routinely regarded as illogical and would entail another weight penalty. HTP-High Test Peroxide- has not been experimented with solely because HTP weighs nearly ten pounds per gallon whereas methanol weighs 6.6 pounds per gallon. Methanol has been used as rocket propellant since World War Two.

The expense and hazards of HTP are more reasons to ignore HTP as a rocket propellant; the hazards are especially severe! However, once suitable fuels are now considered the best fuels to avoid the risks associated with additional experimentation.

Cryogenic oxidizers, such as Liquid Oxygen, pose hazards of their own. Hazards that became well-known early on with rocket experiments completed by Dr. Goddard. Recent disasters caused by chilled gases have happened to SpaceX. The search for more ideal propellants continues after a very long hiatus.

The future of American Space Programs must also include secondary drive systems like angular momentum drives. Anti-gravity drives are still distant in the future as is the notion of having anything other than many nozzles of several rocket engines, but angular momentum drives could assist in take-off and provide maneuvering thrust now. It's amazing that rocket engines alone have kept engineers' content for so long!

Electric motors driving rotating discs would shut down and a decelerating event imposed on the disc would induce a forward thrust vector. The deceleration would stop before excessive angular momentum was used up and the electric motors would start again to rebuild angular momentum.

A series of angular momentum drives about the periphery of the rocket could act as a steering device, and since the thrust vectors generated act on its own frame, asymmetrical forces can accumulate to cause acceleration. VTOLs might be more manageable with more than the rocket engine to control.

Hypersonic missiles have become common for atmospheric munitions deployment. Robotic hypersonic missiles could deliver cargo to the ISS if NASA were so inclined without the cost and suspense of launching an SLS rocket. Smaller, better rockets are inevitable.

The list of improvements that would make American Space Programs better is probably endless and the best improvement might remain unknown. Doubtlessly, the American Space Program in 2040 might not resemble what it is today.

The origin of the improvement might not be predictable or from a dependable source. It might appear as if it came from the most unforeseeable of sources, spontaneously, and without cause. What event will lead towards a huge advancement in any Space Program?

It is good that we have the vastness of Space to explore, the ability to explore it, and, if not the ability to understand it, at least, the skill to marvel at it. Such a necessary skill!

Photography Attributes

All illustrations were sourced from Wikimedia Commons and are represented as "open source" illustrations;

1. File:Dr. Robert H. Goddard - GPN-2002-000131.jpg.

2. File:Hermann Oberth 1950s.jpg.

3. File:Wernher von Braun 1960.jpg.

4. File:Konstantin Tsiolkovsky 1930s2.jpg.

5. File:Fusée V2.jpg.

6. File:Redstone 09.jpg.

7. File:Atlas EELV family.png.

8. File:Apollo 11 Launch - GPN-2000-000630.jpg.

9. File:Super heavy-lift launch vehicles.png.

10. File:STS120LaunchHiRes-edit1.jpg.

11. File:Crew of STS-107, official photo.jpg.

12. File:Challenger flight 51-l crew.jpg.

13. File:Sts et cutaway.jpg.

14. File:SLS Configuration.jpg.

15. By Steve Jurvetson from Menlo Park, USA - SpaceShip Two mated to the Mother ship White Knight Two, CC BY 2.0, https://commons.wikimedia.org/w/index.php?curid=36216747.

16. File:2018-01-28 Stratolaunch Aircraft.png

Image Sources

Dr. Robert Hutchings Goddard

https://www.google.com/url?sa=i&url=https%3A%2F%2Fen.wikipedia.org%2Fwiki%2FRobert_H._Goddard&psig=AOvVaw2xifs94IOPJE-Dhx2BdFuE&ust=1589380633098000&source=images&cd=vfe&ved=0CA0QjhxqFwoTCPC37bLGrukCFQAAAAdAAAAABAD

Robert Albert Charles Esnault-Pelterie

https://www.google.com/url?sa=i&url=https%3A%2F%2Fen.wikipedia.org%2Fwiki%2FRobertEsnault-Pelterie&psig=AOvVaw0m5PRnUv7Oc2bCCF2Kkt3&ust=1589380768706000&source=images&cd=vfe&ved=0CA0QjhxqFwoTCKCJ1fXGrukCFQAAAAdAAAAABAD

Hermann Julius Oberth

https://www.google.com/url?sa=i&url=https%3A%2F%2Fen.wikipedia.org%2Fwiki%2FHermannOberth&psig=AOvVaw02V8NxITZLyKHdaFzCbktE&ust=1589380825634000&source=images&cd=vfe&ved=0CA0QjhxqFwoTCKiLwI7HrukCFQAAAAdAAAAABAD

Wernher Magnus Maximillian, Freiherr von Braun

https://www.google.com/url?sa=i&url=https%3A%2F%2Fen.wikipedia.org%2Fwiki%2FWernher_von_Braun&psig=AOvVaw32jJE18m7XbhY9IRvN9t8R&ust=1589380891693000&source=images&cd=vfe&ved=0CA0QjhxqFwoTCLjhgbDHrukCFQAAAAdAAAAABAD

Konstatin Eduardovich Tsiolkovsky

https://www.google.com/url?sa=i&url=https%3A%2F%2Fen.wikipedia.org%2Fwiki%2FKonstantin_Tsiolkovsky&psig=AOvVaw1FcFWeSgzi1ihfDZWDr43I&ust=1589380947712000&source=images&cd=vfe&ved=0CA0QjhxqFwoTCJihvsnHrukCFQAAAAdAAAAABAE

The V-2 Rocket

https://www.google.com/url?sa=i&url=https%3A%2F%2Fen.wikipedia.org%2Fwiki%2FV-2_rocket&psig=AOvVaw2MgtK-4Qf6783AsZm_AkQ2&ust=1589381008990000&source=images&cd=vfe&ved=0CA0QjhxqFwoTCLjwl-XHrukCFQAAAAAdAAAAABAD

The United States Rocket Program

https://www.google.com/url?sa=i&url=https%3A%2F%2Fwikivisually.com%2Fwiki%2FWRESAT&psig=AOvVaw39bSQG2jlnJk9U4IqWO3EI&ust=1589381258075000&source=images&cd=vfe&ved=0CA0QjhxqFwoTCPjOid3IrukCFQAAAAAdAAAAABAD

The Atlas Rockets Program

https://www.google.com/url?sa=i&url=https%3A%2F%2Flink.springer.com%2Fcontent%2Fpdf%2F10.1007%252F978-3-030-20707-6_82-1.pdf&psig=AOvVaw1edUuZPYXwN0gcpDLu2CYp&ust=1589381345378000&source=images&cd=vfe&ved=0CA0QjhxqFwoTCNCZr4bJrukCFQAAAAAdAAAAABAD

The Saturn 5 Rocket

https://www.google.com/url?sa=i&url=https%3A%2F%2Fen.wikipedia.org%2Fwiki%2FApollo_program&psig=AOvVaw14cyDYo2oXj2oyhTaNC4qc&ust=1589381444916000&source=images&cd=vfe&ved=0CA0QjhxqFwoTCIjJl7XJrukCFQAAAAAdAAAAABAD

Space Shuttle Columbia

https://www.google.com/url?sa=i&url=https%3A%2F%2Fspacelaunchnow.me%2Fvehicle%2Fspacecraft&psig=AOvVaw02JR2k0I99b4STGpngrKT1&ust=1589381667407000&source=images&cd=vfe&ved=0CA0QjhxqFwoTCNjj8KHKrukCFQAAAAAdAAAAABAJ

The lost crew of STS-107
https://www.google.com/url?sa=i&url=https%3A%2F%2Fwww.amazon.com%2FSTS-107-Shuttle-Columbia-Silver-Photo%2Fdp%2FB004G383IS&psig=AOvVaw0O4uDVKats_BfSFe5Zap3Y&ust=1589381957504000&source=images&cd=vfe&ved=0CA0QjhxqFwoTCOjWiK_LrukCFQAAAAAdAAAAABAI

The lost crew of STS-51-L
https://www.google.com/url?sa=i&url=https%3A%2F%2Fen.wikipedia.org%2Fwiki%2FSpace_Shuttle_Challenger_disaster&psig=AOvVaw0N1n12NAbbFcspRZHRqgc3&ust=1589382092206000&source=images&cd=vfe&ved=0CA0QjhxqFwoTCJDjiO3LrukCFQAAAAAdAAAAABBE

The Shuttle External Tank
https://www.google.com/url?sa=i&url=http%3A%2F%2Fwww.mach25media.com%2Fshuttle10.html&psig=AOvVaw0ipODRUtq6LfPuPacW-6GA&ust=1589382449765000&source=images&cd=vfe&ved=0CA0QjhxqFwoTCMjfkJTNrukCFQAAAAAdAAAAABAD

The Super Heavy-Lift Launch Vehicles
https://www.google.com/url?sa=i&url=https%3A%2F%2Fen.wikipedia.org%2Fwiki%2FSuper_heavy-lift_launch_vehicle&psig=AOvVaw33y-TQZ3Rb397M4WsfxDSi&ust=1589382484209000&source=images&cd=vfe&ved=0CA0QjhxqFwoTCJifv6nNrukCFQAAAAAdAAAAABAD

The Space Launch System (SLS)
https://www.google.com/url?sa=i&url=https%3A%2F%2Fwww.nasa.gov%2Fexploration%2Fsystems%2Fsls%2Foverview.html&psig=AOvVaw3v_cgGncMg9mKYFYpWPujG&ust=1589382526502000&source=images&cd=vfe&ved=0CA0QjhxqFwoTCNC_g7zNrukCFQAAAAAdAAAAABAD

VSS Spaceplane

https://www.google.com/url?sa=i&url=https%3A%2F%2Fen.wikipedia.org%2Fwiki%2FVSS_Enterprise&psig=AOvVaw0orEzjdT4E3zfrhsVB2Olg&ust=1589382575476000&source=images&cd=vfe&ved=0CA0QjhxqFwoTCMD_3NTNrukCFQAAAAdAAAAABAD

The Stratolauncher

https://www.google.com/url?sa=i&url=https%3A%2F%2Fcommons.wikimedia.org%2Fwiki%2FFile%3A2018-01-28_Stratolaunch Aircraft_26071200028_6bbee9a16b_o_(crop).jpg&psig=AOvVaw0vndNCdylIM_-mb8H7NcNL&ust=1589382620169000&source=images&cd=vfe&ved=0CA0QjhxqFwoTCODgguvNrukCFQAAAAdAAAAABAI

Printed in the United States
By Bookmasters